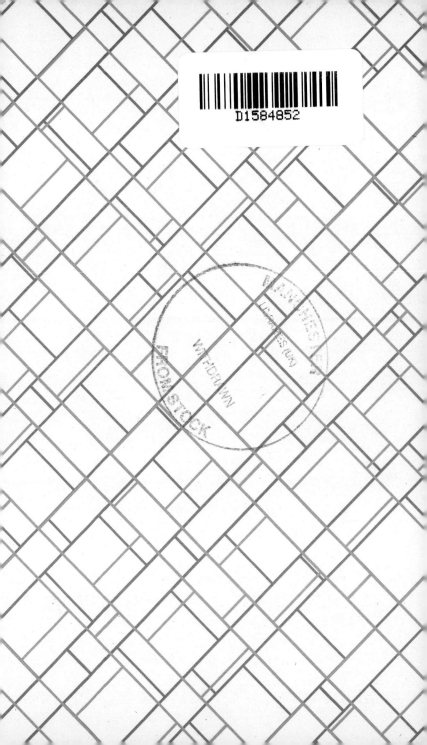

Penguin Readers

ROBIN HOOD

RETOLD BY KAREN KOVACS

LEVEL

S

ILLUSTRATED BY DYNAMO LTD
SERIES EDITOR: SORREL PITTS

PENGUIN BOOKS

UK | USA | Canada | Ireland | Australia
India | New Zealand | South Africa

Penguin Books is part of the Penguin Random House group of companies
whose addresses can be found at global.penguinrandomhouse.com.
www.penguin.co.uk www.puffin.co.uk www.ladybird.co.uk

Penguin Readers edition of *Robin Hood* published by Penguin Books Ltd, 2020
001

Text for Penguin Readers edition adapted by Karen Kovacs
Text for Penguin Readers edition copyright © Penguin Books Ltd, 2020
Illustrated by Dynamo Ltd
Illustrations copyright © Penguin Books Ltd, 2020
Cover illustration by Mary Kate McDevitt

Printed and bound in Great Britain by Clays Ltd, Elcograf S.p.A.

A CIP catalogue record for this book is available from the British Library

ISBN: 978–0–241–46339–0

All correspondence to:
Penguin Books
Penguin Random House Children's
One Embassy Gardens, 8 Viaduct Gardens,
London SW11 7BW

Contents

People in the story   8

New words   10

Before-reading questions   12

Robin Hood   14

During-reading questions   52

After-reading questions   53

Exercises   54

Project work   59

People in the story

the Sheriff
(He works for the King.)

King Richard

Robin Hood

the Merry Men

Little John

New words

archery

catch

contest

forest

hurt

outlaw

poor

rich

winner

Before-reading questions

1 Look at the "New words" on pages 10–11, and complete the sentences in your notebook.

   a She has a lot of money. She is ....

   b He has no money. He is ....

   c .... is a sport.

   d Run! You can .... them.

   e Stop it! Don't .... your brother.

2 Look at the "People in the story" on pages 8–9. Choose two people, and write about them in your notebook.

   a What is his name?

   b What is he wearing?

   c Is he a good or a bad person, do you think?

   d What does he do in the story, do you think?

3 What do you know about Robin Hood?

4 Look at this picture. Who are the men? What are they
doing? Write the answers in your notebook.

Picture definitions of words in **bold** can be found on pages 10–11.

ROBIN HOOD

Sherwood **Forest**, England, in 1193

19

That evening . . .

The Sheriff is angry with me. I'm an **outlaw** now, and the forest is my new home.

Robin Hood finds outlaws in the forest.

One day, Robin Hood is walking in the forest.

Stop.

Why?

This bridge is mine!
You can't walk on it.

25

That afternoon, at some houses near the forest . . .

Robin and his men are in the forest.

No, stop. We don't take money from poor people.

31

Come with me, my men.

33

In 1194, in the town . . .

Archery Contest

Today

The **contest** is starting now.
This money is for the winner.

34

35

He's very good!

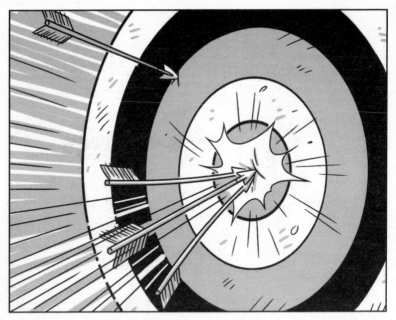

39

41

43

Merry Men, it's me!

51

During-reading questions

Write the answers to these questions in your notebook.

1 Why does the boy kill the animal on page 15?

2 Whose animal is it?

3 Why does Robin Hood help the boy, do you think?

4 Who does Robin Hood find in the forest?

5 Why does Robin Hood laugh on page 25?

6 Look at page 28. Is King Richard in England?
Why is the Sheriff a bad man?

7 On page 33, Robin gives money to poor people.
Where is the money from?

8 Look at page 37. Robin Hood is at the archery contest.
Does the Sheriff know this?

9 Who wins the archery contest?

10 What does Robin Hood do with the money from
the archery contest?

11 Look at pages 42–46. Why does King Richard like
Robin Hood, do you think?

12 Look at pages 43–45. Who is the rich man?

13 Where does Robin Hood go on page 48? Why does he go there?

14 Does Robin Hood like his new work? Why/Why not?

15 On page 51, the Merry Men are happy. Why?

After-reading questions

1 Who is your favourite person in the story? Why are they your favourite person?

2 What is your favourite part of the story? Why is it your favourite part?

3 Do you like the ending of the story?

4 Is Little John a good or bad person, do you think? And is King Richard good or bad?

5 Robin Hood takes money from rich people and gives it to poor people. Is that good or bad, do you think?

Exercises

1 Write these sentences again in your notebook.
Add six capital letters (A, B, C ...), three full stops (.)
and one apostrophe (').

a boy kills an animal in the forest it is king richards animal
the sheriff is angry with him

A....

2 Put these sentences in the correct order in your
notebook.

a .... Little John meets the Merry Men.

b .... Robin Hood finds the Merry Men.

c .... Robin Hood runs from the Sheriff.

d ....*1*..... Robin Hood helps the boy.

e .... Robin Hood gives Little John his name.

f .... Robin Hood meets Little John on the bridge.

3 Complete these sentences in your notebook, using the
words from the box. Who says these sentences?
Example: 1 – a

catch	hurt	winner	contest	outlaw

1 *Catch* him!

2 I'm an .... now.

3 I'm the ....

4 Please don't .... me!

5 Is Robin Hood coming
to the .... ?

a the Sheriff  **b** Robin Hood  **c** Little John

d rich man  **e** poor woman

4 Complete these sentences in your notebook with *a*, *an*, *the* or *Ø* (zero article).

1 ....*Ø*.... Robin Hood is .... outlaw.

2 .... Sheriff is .... bad man.

3 They live in .... England.

4 .... Robin Hood does not take .... money from .... poor people.

5 There is .... archery contest today.

6 This money is for .... winner.

5 **Correct these sentences in your notebook.**

1 The archery contest is in the forest.
The archery contest is in the town.

2 Robin Hood is not at the contest.

3 Robin Hood gives the money to his Merry Men.

4 King Richard talks to Robin Hood at the contest.

5 The Sheriff catches Robin Hood.

6 **Which five words from the story have silent letters
(= you don't say these letters)? Write the five words
and <u>underline</u> the silent letters in your notebook.**
Example: _wa<u>l</u>k_

1 walk   **5** John

2 king   **6** Robin

3 look   **7** know

4 friend   **8** listen

7 **Complete these sentences in your notebook with the
correct form of the verb.**

1 I _am_ (be) Robin Hood.

2 Robin Hood .... (find) outlaws in the forest.

3 One day, Robin Hood .... (walk) in the forest.

56

4 This bridge is mine! You can't .... (walk) on it.

5 No, Sheriff. Please, ... (not take) my money.

6 Oh, thank you, Robin! You .... (help) us again.

8 Complete these sentences in your notebook, using the words from the box.

| his | hers | yours | mine | theirs |

1 You can't kill King Richard's animals. They are _his_, not ....

2 Don't walk on this bridge. It's ....

3 The Sheriff is taking that money, but it's .... They are very angry with him.

4 You can't have that woman's goat. It's ....

9 Look at the picture on page 49, and answer the questions in your notebook.

1 What is Robin Hood doing?

2 Does he like it?

3 Why/Why not?

4 Where does he go?
What does he do there?

10 Match the two parts of the sentences in your notebook.

Example: *1 – d*

1	Robin Hood is	**a**	catch Robin Hood.
2	The Merry Men	**b**	hurt people.
3	The Sheriff cannot	**c**	is the winner.
4	Robin Hood does not	**d**	very good at archery.
5	The Merry Men are	**e**	live in Sherwood Forest.
6	At the contest, Robin Hood	**f**	outlaws.

Project work

1 Robin Hood is talking to you:

Come and live with me and my Merry Men in the forest.

You can take five things with you to the forest. What do you take, and why?

2 You are one of the Merry Men. Write about a day with Robin Hood.

3 You find £10,000 in the street. You tell the police, but they do not want it. What do you do with the money? Talk about your answers.
- Do you give it to a friend, to a person in your family or to poor people?
- Or is it for you? What can you buy with the money?

4 Choose a rich person from your country. Make a poster.
- Put photos of the rich person on the poster.
- What is his/her name?
- How old is he/she?
- How does he/she make money?
- What does he/she do with his/her money?
- Does he/she help poor people?
- Is he/she a good person, do you think?

An answer key for all questions and exercises can be found at **www.penguinreaders.co.uk**

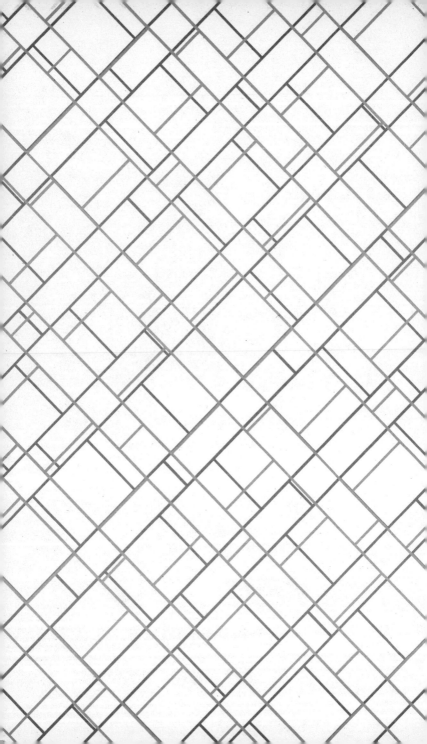

Penguin 🐧 **Readers**

Visit **www.penguinreaders.co.uk**
for FREE Penguin Readers resources
and digital and audio versions of this book.